MEN OF
THE OPEN
RANGE

& *other poems*

MIKE LOGAN

Men of the Open Range, oil painting by
Charles M. Russell, courtesy Mackay Collection,
Montana Historical Society.

Library of Congress Catalog Card Number: 93-72958
ISBN: 1-56044-247-6

Published by Buglin' Bull Press, in cooperation with
SkyHouse Publishers, an imprint of Falcon Press
Publishing Co., Inc., Helena, Montana.

Photography by Mike Logan

Design, typesetting, and other prepress work
by Laurie "gigette" Gould
Falcon Graphics, Helena, Montana.

Distributed by Buglin' Bull Press and by Falcon Press
Publishing Co., Inc., P.O. Box 1718, Helena, Montana 59624,
or call 1-800-582-2665.

Additional copies of
Men of the Open Range are available by
sending $7.95 plus $1.50 postage
and handling to Buglin' Bull Press,
32 S. Howie, Helena, MT 59601.

Buglin' Bull Press
32 S. Howie, Helena, MT 59601

First Edition
Manufactured in the United States of America.

Dedication

This book is dedicated to Bruce and Pauline Benson, their daughters Evelyn and Valerie, and to Fred and Dot Benson of the X BAR LAZY M in Avon and Deer Lodge. Without their encouragement, patience, and, most of all, their friendship and hospitality, a lot of my poems would never have been written and a lot of my pictures would never have been taken. No one could ask for better friends.

Foreword

In the West, the essence of the story was, and still is, in the telling. Blackfeet lodge tales and Salish legends of the fall set the standard in the years "when the land belonged to God." Certainly the likes of Bret Harte, Mark Twain, Owen Wister, Frederic Remington, and Charlie Russell captured in words or on canvas what the West was like in its early settlement days. D. J. O'Malley, Badger Clark, and Curley Fletcher, too, added their two cents by using a "new twist" in verse and rhyme. That tradition of the well-told, skillfully rendered story remains with us today, particularly in cowboy poetry.

Today's cowboy poets, the Mike Logans of Montana and the North American West, are the bearers of that tradition and the chroniclers of *our* times. Mike's poems are studied, not so much in the academic sense, but in his intimate familiarity with the style, the techniques, and perhaps, most important, the traditions of the West. His crafting of words perks your ears and your senses; they're up like a horse's when he catches a glimpse of something curious from the corner of his eye. Mike's uncanny ability to use and play with meter and rhyme, combined with a healthy dosage of old-time language—words and slang—creates brush strokes to paint the story. Interwoven is humor, sentiment, experience, and familiarity with the western way of life. These elements set his poems in motion like colors dancing in the northern lights.

Mike's work shows that real quality poetry is not just "moon, june, spoon..." slopped out with some superficial trappings. There is art, there is thought, and there is simple elegance in Mike's poetry.

Many are the times that Mike has called me, late in the evening, with a new poem he's written. Often, he'd preface his story with, "I don't know if you're gonna like what I say here, but...." I've always replied, "I may not like *what* you say, but I'll like *how* you say it."

With this book, Mike mixes his own metaphors by combining his words and stories with his images and photographs. My only regret with his change of illustrators is that when people hold up the book with the Charlie Russell painting on the cover, cock one eyebrow, and ask incredulously, "You illustrated this?" I will no longer be able to say in sincere half truth, "Yes, I did."

I think you'll like a lot of what Mike says and how he says it.

Mike Korn

Acknowledgments

The author would like to thank the following publications, in which some of the poems were first published.

Bugle: "Elk Camp"

Cowboy Magazine: "The Code" and "Cowboy Lighthouse"

Dry Crik Review: "Hollywood and Vine" and "Letter to Town"

Montana Stockgrower: "Late Again"

Introduction

It is my pleasure, once again, through the kindness of the Montana Historical Society, to use one of my favorite Charlie Russell paintings, *Men of the Open Range,* on the cover of this book.

I truly think that, to Charlie Russell, "to ride the far sung places and to hear the west wind sing was to know the horseman's Holy Grail."

Several times, I have had people tell me that the pinks, purples, and golds in this and other of Charlie's works do not exist in nature. My reply has always been that if they think that, they haven't been there.

I tend to go on the fight a bit when people move to Montana and *immediately* want to change "our high pure mountain valleys to somethin' not so different from L.A. streets and alleys." I came to Big Sky Country twenty-five years ago and our way of life here is near heaven for me. Most Montanans like our state the way it is and do not relish seeing it changed.

A word of explanation might be in order for "Fiddlin' Sam." Maiden is a ghost town near Lewistown, and the "prayer books" referred to are what the old time cowboys called their little books of cigarette papers. In the poem "If Spanish is the Lovin' Tongue," the Spanish words are usually given the original pronunciation.

My special thanks to Mike Korn for "riding shotgun" for me once again, this time in words. I'm not sure I would have felt right doing a book of poems without Mike having some part of it. I'm proud to call him my friend.

My deepest gratitude also to my friends, Darrell Arnold, Guy Logsdon, Gwen Petersen, Tom Eaton, and Baxter Black for the kind comments on the back of the book. I value their friendship far more than silver or gold. As Baxter put it in his insightful poem, "Take Care of Your Friends,"

All worldly riches and tributes of men
Can't hold a candle to the worth of a friend.

Thanks to Wally McRae, Paul Zarzyski, and my wife, Judy, for listening so patiently, and to old friends whose lives and ways have meant so much to me.

Mike Logan
Helena, Montana 1993

Contents

Contents continued

Men of the Open Range

I can see the ghosts of riders
Movin' out across the dawn.
The gold of day's first comin'
Paints their passin', then they're gone.

They were men of open ranges.
No wire cut their kingdom then.
They rode as knights on grassland oceans.
Lords, beyond the townsman's ken.

They made circles on the rangelands
Eagle wild and dog wolf free.
Bounded only by horizons,
Flung so far no eye could see.

I can hear the leather creakin'
And the jinglin' of the spurs
And the whisperin' of hoofbeats
And the hiss of lucifers

As they're lightin' up the makin's
On the way to gather cows
In the breaks of the Big Muddy
With the freedom God allows

Only to the few, the chosen,
To the horsemen on the land
Where a man could see the elephant
Or know his Maker's hand.

They could be both proud and humble
For the gift of sky and space
That would make those unfamiliar
Fear the vastness of the place.

They were men who'd trade no other,
Be he commoner or king,
For to ride the far sung places
And to hear the west wind sing

Was to know the horseman's Holy Grail
Know paradise each morning
Where horse was gift of God to man
And yet to know the warning

That all could change, that all could change
Beyond the nightmares they might see.
That men could come with plows and fences
Like some plague, could steal their free

And easy rides out in the dawning,
Steal their wild and open range.
Steal the jingle from their spurs and
Ring their death knell with the change.

But these were men of open ranges.
No wire cut their kingdom then.
They rode as knights on grassland oceans
Lords, beyond the townsman's ken.

I can see the ghosts of riders
Movin' out across the dawn.
The gold of day's first comin'
Paints their passin'. Now they're gone.

Fiddlin' Sam

Boys is ridin' up to Maiden
Though they ain't exactly laden
With the riches of the realm, as some might say.
Still they think they'll do some prancin'
And some old time country dancin'.
Ain't a thought of headin' home 'til break of day.

But, them boys is plumb dismayed
At a grievous error made
In the hurry up to hit the trail that night.
When they pass the makin's 'round
Nary lucifer is found.
Not a ranahan can wrangle up a light.

Well, them boys is in a fix,
'Cause, short of rubbin' sticks,
Ain't a chance of findin' fire for twenty mile.
And the thought of buildin' smokes
With no sulfurs in their pokes
Ain't a thing that's likely bringin' on no smile.

So they're took some by surprise
When they top this little rise
To find ol' Fiddlin' Sam just hangin' there,
Swayin' right smart in the breeze,
That's a soughin' through the trees,
Like some ballroom dandy treadin' light on air.

Sam was always fond of fiddlin'
And his voice was fair to middlin'
'Til this necktie party starts him on the swing.
Must 'a' tripped the light fantastic
Though he weren't enthusiastic.
Stretched that hemp as tight as any fiddle string.

Boys ain't feelin' much remorse,
'Cause they, each one, knowed, of course,
Of ol' Sam's well-knowed propensity to steal.
And he, special, favored hosses,
So to cut their cavvy losses,
The cowmen made an offer plumb genteel.

They said, "Sam, you rattle hocks
'Cause there won't be no more talks.
If we see you on this range again, you'll swing."
But the word has filtered down,
From a dance, last week in town,
That ol' Fiddlin' Sam was there to play and sing.

While this deal's some bad for Sam,
Still them boys is in a jam
And they know it wouldn't raise the fiddler's ire
If they rifled through his vest
In their pyrotechnic quest.
Where ol' Sam is headed there is beaucoup fire.

When they fish Sam's matches out
Them boys break that smokin' drought
With a will that shore approaches plumb good cheer.
Well, their prayer books is devout
And of thanks there ain't no doubt
But they're kind of wishin' Sam had had some beer.

While they all enjoy this smoke,
Still they're goin' to Maiden broke
When sudden like, this boy lets out a hoot.
Says, "Ol' Sam he had this stash,
Just a bit of ready cash
And he always kept it hid out in his boot!!"

So, respectful like and slow,
Though ol' Sam'd never know,
They sidles up and takes 'im by the heel.
That boot it slides off easy
And the boys is feelin' queasy
As they tip it up to have a cautious feel.

But their fear and trepidation
Turns to instant jubilation
As this shiny double eagle hits the ground.
And it seems to them a sign
That, ol' Sam, he wouldn't mind
Them a usin' this bonanza that they found.

They spurs out of there, anon,
Once they slip Sam's boot back on.
Wouldn't want their benefactor catchin' cold.
And there's merriment and song,
As our heroes ride along,
'Cause they're headed into Maiden flush with gold.

Well, they hit the dance on time
And the music it's sublime.
The fiddle's makin' extra special sounds.
And, somehow, it seems just right,
As they're dancin' through the night,
That it's Fiddlin' Sam that's buyin' all the rounds.

This poem is dedicated to Homer Loucks,
who told me the story.

Cowboy Lighthouse

Did you ever see a cowboy
With his hat off in the sun?
Reflections off his forehead
Could make wild horses run.

Its alabaster flashin's
Could put antelope to flight
Or stun a rock guitarist
With the brilliance of its light.

If you could get a candle
To shine on him just right,
A cowboy'd make a lighthouse
For the blackest stormy night.

But this is pure quill guesswork,
When all is said and done,
'Cause you won't see no *real* cowboy
With his hat off in the sun.

Free Verse Bronc Rider

That free verse bronc rider, Zarzyski,
Weren't feelin', one go, none too frisky.
He'd drawed a bad *horse*,
For non-rhymers of *course*,
'Cause, that ol' bronc's name it was Whiskey!!

The Code

There's a code the old westerner lived by.
He called it "THE CODE OF THE WEST."
That code was as real to the cowboy
As his hat or his gun or his vest.

It laid out the rules of the rangelands
Though it wasn't set down in a book.
It lived in the heart of the cowboy,
Rode herd on each action he took.

It was carved, by the winds, on the high buttes.
It was burned on the range by the sun.
It was, sometimes, learned at a hangin' tree
Or taught by the roar of a gun.

A man never spoke "THE CODE OF THE WEST."
He'd 'a' had a hard time with the words.
He just went and lived it the best that he could
Out on the range with the herds.

A cowboy had to have sand in his craw,
True grit when he had to be tough.
Hell, that was expected, 'cause life it was hard.
He smiled when the going got rough.

He didn't complain when a blizzard hit
Or he rode for days without rest
Or turned a stampede or buried a pard,
That was part of "THE CODE OF THE WEST."

A man didn't need watching over.
His calling was a matter of pride.
He worked just the same by his lonesome
As he did with the boss at his side.

A puncher was loyal to his outfit.
He'd stick by his brand to the end.
He was tongue-tied and gentle with women.
He never went back on a friend.

"THE CODE" was unyielding as granite.
It said that you treat a man square.
You didn't backshoot if it came to a fight.
You gave him a chance that was fair.

A cowman talked straight and was honest.
His handshake might buy a man's herd.
No lawyers or contracts, just gave him his hand.
A man was as good as his word.

So, here's to that old time cowboy code.
It still lives out here in the West.
The world might find if it tried it today
That cow country code's still the best.

Letter to Town

I thought I'd write you folks in town
Who like to eat good beef,
But if the price goes up two cents
Are plumb prostrate with grief.

You don't like poison'n' gophers
That's eatin' my best grass
Or shootin' grizzle bears 'r wolves,
Endangered now, alas!!

I wonder how your tunes'd change
If gophers chewed your lawns
Or ol' griz ate your poodle dogs?
What then the pros 'n cons?

Now, just say all them "experts"
Said, "Shoot, boys, let's be fair.
We'll interduce them bears in town,
Ol' griz once lived right there!"

You think ol' Cleveland Am'ry
Or the D O double U*
Would want them bears in *their* backyards?
That's just what *I* thought too!!

I think a stack o' snowballs
All piled up in July
Would last purt' near ten times as long
An' shorthorn bulls'd fly,

Before ol' Am'ry an' his crowd
Would deign to come around
An' learn t' play Adopt-a-Bear,
At least on their home ground.

Now, understand, they'd like that game
If they could use *my* place,
But bring them critters back in town?
They'd laugh right in yer face.

So, next time when them "experts"
Says, "Boys here's what we'll do....."
You stop and think if this new plan
Is one you'd want near *you!*

D.O.W.- Defenders of Wildlife

If Spanish is the Lovin' Tongue

If Spanish is the lovin' tongue
It's also "talkin' cow."
The Mexican vaqueros
Is the ones that taught us how

To work the herds and what to call
The things we didn't know.
Their words flowed north plumb natural
From down in Mexico.

The "cow talk" starts with Cortez
And his three crosses brand.
Those first cows in the New World
Soon crossed the Rio Grande.

The longhorns calved like rabbits
And in a few short years
The new lands up in Texas
Was flooded with slick ears.

The lingo them vaqueros spoke
Made words we savvy now.
If Spanish is the lovin' tongue
It's also "talkin' cow."

There's music in the way they talked
And, though we changed the words,
The liltin' sound of Mexico
Rolled north with Texas herds.

McCartys, taps and theodores
And stampedes in the night;
Mecates, tapaderos,
Fiadores said it right.

Caballada changed to cavvy.
The remuda meant the same.
And coonies cradled cow chips
'Neath the camp cook's wagon frame.

Coyote, lobo, bronco
The brushed up cimarrón
Whether said of men or cattle
They was better left alone.

Jáquimas y dar la vuelta
We changed the way they're said.
Hackamores and dallies
Is the words we used instead.

La reata was a lass rope.
Chigaderos we call chinks.
Zorrillas, black and white cows,
Chihuahuas always clinks.

Rodeo's a money game
The cowboy is the star.
Rodeo is the roundup,
It comes from rodear.

Mesteño was a mustang
Pinto a painted hoss.
Grullas, palominos, too.
The caporal was boss.

Chaps was short for chapareras
Or leggin's for the brush.
They was born in the brasada
Where men plowed through in a rush.

Ladino named the outlaw cow.
Cinchas held the leather throne.
Tapaojos was eye covers
And a sheltered spot, rincón.

Látigo y cuarta
Or, sometimes, el romal,
A stock whip called chicote
Workin' cows in el corral.

A chileno is a ring bit
Hondos slip the runnin' noose.
The man who knows las vacas
Savvies well the lazo's use.

A cow or horse is locoed.
Caponera's from capón.
For goodbyes to a sweetheart,
Adiós, mi corazón.

If Spanish is the lovin' tongue.
It's also "talkin' cow."
Muchas gracias, vaqueros.
You're the ones that taught us how.

Mr. Magpie

Well, he flies like he's been drinkin'
An' his rudder's out of whack.
Kind of waffles 'crost the valley
Then teeter totters back.

Tuxedoed up plumb elegant,
In white and shiny black,
Mr. Magpie dines, fastidious,
On any roadkill snack.

On deepwoods bits of carrion
He'll strut and preen and brag
And put away a gourmet feast
That'd make a maggot gag.

But while most folks revile him
As a noisy garbage eater
He's got this great redeeming trait.
He leaves the place some neater.

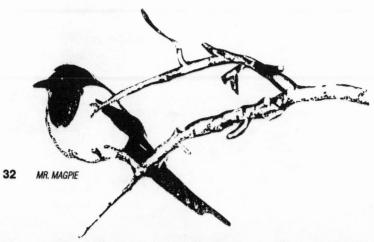

Cowboy Cruise Control

These boys, they ain't plumb housebroke yet.
Ain't used t' modern ways.
They've read about them rodeos.
The money that they pays.

Them stories in the *Horseman*
Has hooked 'em right enough.
The champ, he's just a little squirt.
It cain't be all that tough.

So ridin' off the rimrocks
They thinks they'll do 'er right.
They'll get a brand new travel van
An' save on airplane flight.

They stops at this here RV place
An' sees this fancy van.
In less time than a doggin' run
Up pops this new car man.

This feller, he's plumb friendly.
He's grinnin' like a whelp.
He howdies 'em like long lost pards.
Cain't hardly wait t' help.

That van, it's got them captain's seats,
A well-stocked little bar
An' lots of shiny doodads.
They ain't plumb shore what are.

There's two TV's, a VCR
An' skylights overhead,
A stereo and tapedeck.
It's even got a bed.

There's automatic windows.
No need to turn no crank,
An' with that car thief warnin'
It's safe as any bank.

There's readin' lights an' cruise control
An' window seats galore.
The air conditioner keeps it cool.
There's carpets on the floor.

The salesman takes 'em for a ride
Out on the interstate.
Its lanes is straight as new built fence
Our heroes think it's great.

He slips 'er into cruise control
An' shows 'em how to do it.
Then sits there talkin', plumb relaxed.
It's plain, ain't nothin' to it.

He shows 'em 'bout the stereo
An' that new VCR.
Claims they can see their rides played back
Just like some movie star.

So, now, they'll share the travel costs,
Hit ever' show they can.
They spend their whole life's savin's
On this chromed-up travel van.

That car man, he goodbyes 'em
With handshakes all around.
An' now our future cowboy stars
Is headed out of town.

They'll hit the show in Wolf Point
The old Wild Horse Stampede.
That new van's gassed and rarin'.
They'll try 'er out for speed.

They're headed out on Highway 3,
A road they always traveled,
But on the bend just north of town.
Things starts to come unraveled.

The boy that's drivin', he gets up
An' heads back t' the bar.
T' build hisself a whisky ditch
But he don't get that far.

'Cause when he sets that cruise control
They run right off the bend.
Before they're out of town good,
Their plans is at a end.

He never got t' build no drink.
The van's a awful wreck.
Looks like some big ol' beetle
That crashed and broke his neck.

You know that number nine one one?
Run over quick and dial it.
Turns out that boy thought cruise control
Was automatic pilot.

Peace on Earth

Here's hopin' that the Christ Child
Looks down on you today
And brings you health and happiness
And loved ones on the way

To gather at your table
As you celebrate His birth.
May He guide and bless our country
And grant true peace on earth.

Few Words

His first day on the outfit
This boy don't raise no row.
You know right quick by watchin'
He's no stranger to the cow.

He does the things that's needed
An' the way he does 'em's right,
But the ol' big augur's with us
An' he's some on the fight.

The ol' man he's a pawin' dirt.
Tells this boy, pushin' some,
"I'm a man of mighty few words.
If I say come, you come."

This new hand he don't scare much.
He stops an' builds a smoke.
You see the way he eyes the boss
He ain't plumb gentle broke.

"Well, I'm a man of few words too.
Don't even do much hummin'.
You see me shake my head for no,
You'll savvy I ain't comin'."

Gone

The humpbacked beef is all gone now.
His millions all fell to the gun.
The elk's all pulled back to the mountains,
No more the high prairies to run.

The wolf and the grizzly's near memories
From times when they culled the great herds
And Blackfeet, Cheyenne and Shoshone
Ain't warriors, just old timey words.

They've dammed all the free rollin' rivers
That served as the highways, back when.
Gone are the jerk line muleskinners.
Gone are the wild mountain men.

They've turned all the sod on the cow trails.
The grass is all under wire.
Gone are the old open ranges
That made the great cattle empire.

The cowboy don't follow the wagon today.
Camp cooks is a thing of the past.
The old time rep ain't needed no more.
The nighthawks has all sung their last.

Bluff

Ol' Fred steps out to close the gate
An' chuckles as he passes,
"This shore looks like a workin' truck."
It's plain he don't need glasses.

I glance around the pickup bed.
I'm ridin' on the back.
From where I'm sittin' looks to me
Like ol' Fred's right on track.

There's post hole diggers, hayforks,
Bob wire an' hog wire too
Some staples an' four fenceposts
A sledge that ain't real new.

Three teeth from off a dump rake
Some harness and a kak
Six *Livestock Market Digests*
All turned to Baxter Black

Two bales of straw, a high boy jack
A piece of old saw log
A tool box 'n a chain saw blade
An' one ol' heelin' dog.

Three irrigatin' shovels,
A bottle of propane,
Two purt' near used up plastic tarps
An one ol' broke tire chain.

That glance around the pickup bed
Spells "workin' truck" sure 'nuff.
Ol' Fred he grins at me then winks
An' says, "It's all a bluff."

The Young Cowboy's Story

THE OLD SONG:

As I walked out in the streets of Laredo,
As I walked out in Laredo one day,
I spied a young cowboy all wrapped in white linen,
All wrapped in white linen as cold as the clay.

"I see by your outfit that you are a cowboy,"
These words he did say as I boldly stepped by;
"Come sit down beside me and hear my sad story,
I'm shot in the breast and I'm going to die."

THE STORY:

I sat down beside him, that lonesome young
   cowboy,
All wrapped in white linen and shot in the breast.
And as he lay dyin' he told me this story,
As old as cowboyin', as old as the West.

"We've gathered a herd in the breaks of the Bravo,
Across the great river from old Mexico.
In sight of Laredo we've worked 'em and branded.
We're mostly young cowboys all rarin' to go.

With two thousand head of road-branded longhorns
The outfit's all set to pull out the next day.
We're leavin' Laredo and bound for the railhead
In far off Dodge City, two hard months away.

On good grass and water, the cows are plumb
   peaceful
And even the rounders have all bedded down.
The boss gives the nod for us boys not on night
   guard
To hit the cantinas our last night in town.

Before he's through noddin', we're saddled and
   ridin'.
We're off to Laredo to see all the sights
And, feelin' some playful, we race down the main
   street
A whoopin' n' hollerin' n' shootin' at lights.

I spur for the card-house to play me some monte.
The barkeep don't smile when I ride right on in.
The marshal he's testy 'cause we come a shootin'
He warns me partic'lar, "Don't do it again."

He says I should tie up outside at the hitch rack
An' keep my gun holstered til I'm out of town.
I get me some whiskey and head for the tables.
Things start goin' bad from the time I sit down.

My luck it's all colder 'n a snake in a norther.
Ain't seen a good card since I took my first hand.
'Fore too long, I'm busted and, braved up on
    whiskey,
I'm lured down the street by a Mexican band.

I head for the back door of Rosa's Cantina
And my dark eyed Maria to ask for a dance.
I find her all wrapped in the arms of another.
The love in her eyes tells I ain't got a chance.

But though the floor's buckin' and my gait's
    unsteady,
I try to cut in at the end of the song.
The cowboy that's waltzin' Maria refuses.
I go on the fight though I know I'm dead wrong.

I'm in a black mood 'cause of bad cards and whiskey
And now my Maria has been took away.
I go for my gun and this young puncher shoots me.
I'll never see Dodge 'cause I'm dyin' today."

Well, this is the story that young cowboy told me
His life ebbin' slowly, those long years ago,
And with his last breath, he asked me this favor.
Down 'crost the great river from old Mexico.

THE OLD SONG:

"Get six husky cowboys to carry my coffin,
Get ten lovely maidens to sing me a song,
And beat the drum slowly and play the fife lowly,
For I'm a young cowboy who knows he was wrong."

We beat the drum slowly and played the fife lowly,
And wept in our grief as we bore him along,
For we loved the cowboy, so brave and so handsome,
We loved that young cowboy although he'd done
    wrong.

Nash

I bought two cows and then a dog.
That used up all my cash.
I never had no horse to ride.
I gathered with my Nash.

Celebration

A windsong woke the wildflowers
Up the Middle Fork today.
He whispered to the paintbrush,
"Ruth Korell has gone away."

"I think I'll hum a happy tune,"
The gentle zephyr said,
"For all the times she rode up here
And gave old Sox her head."

"She knew where they were going
Each time they took a ride."
The crocus told the shooting stars
That nodded at his side.

The harebell added proudly,
"I was happy when she came.
She loved to ride Sox up the trail
And tell the guests my name."

Up spoke the wild geranium,
His leaves still wet with dew.
"I was her favorite wildflower.
The guests all knew me, too."

Today, the windsong's melodies
Fill trails Ruth rode along
And, like that warming west wind,
We'll sing a happy song.

Ruth left her brand forever,
As mother, friend and wife,
On Charlie Russell country.
She lived here all her life.

We'll think of all the good times
Down at the Circle Bar.
The dances and the music and
The guests who came so far

To know the hospitality
That Biddie and her Bill
Just seemed to make as natural
As sunlight on a hill.

They partnered fifty-seven years,
As man and loving wife,
To raise four kids and build a ranch.
A full and happy life.

Bill never walked when he could run.
No time to sit and dream.
She'd never rest when she could work.
A fine high-stepping team.

She always got up early.
"Up, boys!" to Jake and Phil.
"You can't just sit around all day."
Time wasn't meant to kill.

As tough as sun-dried rawhide,
As gentle as a dove,
To Colleen and to Isabelle
Their mother's name was love.

Ruth topped her class in high school,
Played basketball as well.
Work habits learned beside their mom
Helped all her kids excel.

She'd quote, if you were feeling low
And said, "Nobody cares,"
"The elevator to success
Is broken, take the stairs."

She liked to watch as Sarah
Built up the Circle Bar.
A showplace for Montana,
A guest ranch without par.

Ruth saw the throng in Utica
That held her state so dear.
She got to help us celebrate
Montana's hundredth year.

I think Ruth's looking down today
From heaven's highest hill.
She's prob'ly sitting on old Sox
And holding hands with Bill.

Heaven's prob'ly running smoother
Since Ruth Korell is there.
You know those angels don't sleep late
And each one does his share.

As that gentle windsong whispered,
"Ruth Korell has gone away."
But if heaven has a guest ranch
Up near the milky way

Biddie's prob'ly got it running
Just like the Circle Bar
And there's music and there's dancing
And there's trails up to some star

Where she can take a trail ride,
With angels all in tow,
To show them heaven's wildflowers
Where golden zephyrs blow.

*This poem was written for a memorial service for
Ruth Korell, pioneer ranch woman in the Utica area.
It is dedicated to her daughters, Colleen and Isabelle,
and to her sons, Phil and Jake.*

Elk Camp

There's no place as near to heaven
As where I am right now.
An elk camp in the Rockies
Is plumb close anyhow.

From my old down sack I hear a bull
Makin' war talk to the moon.
Purty soon ol' Cooky'll sing out
His old familiar tune.

"Up boys them bulls is waitin'
An' you gotta have your chuck.
We got some trackin' snow last night.
I think you're plumb in luck."

Now some folks like angelic choirs
An' harps that's played on high,
But if heaven ain't got elk camps,
Well, I think I'll pass it by.

Hollywood and Vine

Them movie moguls like to shoot
Out here where they can see
The blueness of the Big Sky
And mountains high and free.

Them actors always love this land
Where streams run clear and clean
And men still ranch ahorseback
And towns ain't coarse and mean.

So most of them big film stars
Brag up our Treasure State
And say they'd like to live here
'Cause city life they hate.

They buy up lots of ranches,
Raise elk and buffalo.
Or, better yet, they subdivide
For "ranchettes" don't you know.

We seem to need enlightening
'Bout "Guccis", "Kleins" and such.
Us poor benighted savages
Just ain't been kept in touch

With subtle civilizin' things
Like drugs and modern traumas.
We tend to lean toward simpler things
Like Coors and Tony Lamas.

But them "New Wavers" cowboy up
And plumb turn missionaries
To bring us all them "rad" new things
That they deem "necessaries."

And, pretty soon, their zeal has changed
Our high pure mountain valleys
To somethin' not so different
From L. A. streets and alleys.

Now if they like conveniences
Of city life so fine,
Why don't the sonsabitches stay
At Hollywood and Vine?

Late Again

The sun's been down an hour
An' we're long overdue.
The kitchen light's still burnin'
And Pauline? She is too.

We left her at the dump rake
A full three hours ago.
"We're goin' to check the spring at Spears'.
Be back before you know."

"Well, supper's almost ready.
Try not to be too long."
"It won't take but a minute."
I think she's heard this song.

The hayin' crew's all starvin'
They're headed in, you see.
By that I mean the whole darn bunch,
Except for Bruce and me.

We check the spring at Spears' place
And fix a little fence
Then up to see a work horse colt
The sun, it's down long since.

We shed our hats and muddy boots
And stockin' foot it in.
But walkin' soft don't make it.
We're caught. Plumb late again.

Ol' Bruce he gets this sheepy look,
Slides in beside his plate.
An' me, I'm playin' invisible.
It ain't fun bein' late.

The kitchen it's some chilly
The food ain't really hot
An' Bruce's stammerin' some excuse,
But we both know we're caught.

We'll put on this united front,
List all the work we done.
An' faced with Pauline's silent stare
We'll bear this blame as one.

We'll be like old time saddle pards
Fort up for this attack
An' go down guns a blazin',
Each guard the other's back.

Pauline sets out the roast beef
Ol' Bruce says, "Pass the salt."
An' like some yeller tweety bird
I sing, "It's Bruce's fault."

Drinkers of the Wind (Pronghorns)

Sprinters of the sage,
Who scan with eagled eyes,
Their wild untreed horizons.
Watchers on the rise.

Phantoms of the snow,
Who take on shadowed form,
And hunch before the blizzard's rage.
Endurers of the storm.

Drinkers of the wind,
Who, running, seem to fly,
Across a boundless short grass plain.
Racers to the sky.

Children of the sun,
Who, when the prairie roasts,
Become, beneath that blazing orb,
Dust-deviled dancing ghosts.

Second Flat

I'm a hunderd miles from nowhere
When I get this second flat.
As I stop to look it over
The windgod grabs my hat.

Well, he whirls it down the gravel
'Til it doesn't have much brim.
I'm doin' eighty when I catch it
Runnin' on that right rear rim.

The other tires is flat, now
The fire has got 'em all
'Cause the hay that I was haulin'
Caught a spark to start the ball.

The engine it's a blazin'
An' my moustache it caught too
An' my glass left eye's a meltin'
An' I ain't sure what to do.

Well, my heeler clears the window
Just in time to miss the blast
When that red hot rim makes contact
With a bit of leakin' gas.

I never see my hat again.
I had to look away
An' my good eye it's a water'n'
Like a irrigatin' spray.

Probl'y went to South Dakota
Or maybe Ioway.
The speed was supersonic
It was headed that a way.

The Other Choice

Happy birthday, Pardner.
We're longer in the tooth
By twelve full moons than last year.
We're both some past our youth.

We cain't ride like we used to.
Cain't sit our hoss as well.
Need cheaters when we read a brand,
But, Pard, we'll never tell.

We'll count up all our blessin's
An' read this birthday verse.
We don't like gettin' older,
But the other choice is worse.

Calf

Well, he's just a little feller.
Ain't yet got the strength to beller
And he's kind of wobbly legged at the knees.
He was born in a March blizzard,
Cold enough to freeze your gizzard,
But his mammy found 'im shelter in the trees.

Well at first he don't know much,
But he savvies mammy's touch
And his teeter totter'n' get up's plumb absurd.
Soon he gets the hang of walkin',
Learns his mammy's way of talkin'
So he'll know 'er from the far side of the herd.

He's bright-eyed as a camp robber
With his face all caked with slobber.
A feller'd have to say he's quite a mess.
But he's healthy and alert,
This rambunctious little squirt,
And his antics cause his mammy some distress.

He'll shore kick up quite a fuss,
This demandin' little cuss,
If his ma ain't there to feed 'im when it's time.
Soon he's racin' with the others,
Lots of them is his half brothers,
Always lookin' for a bigger hill to climb.

All this cute's just incidental.
Naw, we don't get sentimental.
No sense a feller makin' lots of noise.
Ain't no need to sing or shout,
But *he's* what it's all about.
He's the lifeblood of the cattle country, boys.

That Wally McRae

It created quite a sensation
At that gath'rin' from all 'round the nation.
That Wally McRae,
From up Montana way,
Was teachin' 'bout "reincarnation"!!

A Droughty Christmas

Here's hopin' ol' Dad Christmas
Is wearin' his fireproof boots.
If your camp's half as dry as ours
He'll need asbestos suits.

I shore do hope them reindeer
Ain't shod with iron this year
When Santy's makin' all his rounds
To spread his yuletide cheer.

You know that sled's a throwin' sparks
Each time he touches down.
It's bad as strikin' matches
When them runners hits the ground.

The range is dryer'n camel spit
Or Scrooge's dried up heart.
Reflections off a horned toad's eye
Could get a blaze to start.

But, shoot, the kids is all prepared,
With lots of reindeer food
An' milk an' fancy cookies.
So it'd be plumb rude

To wave 'im off on Christmas Eve
All loaded down with toys
An' maybe ruin the joy he brings
To little girls and boys.

So wet down ever' gunny sack
That you can lay a hand on
Shoot, maybe, it bein' Christmas,
He'll bring some snow to land on.

Plane Tough

I'm headed home from Elko.
Ain't slept in near five days.
I ain't much fond of flyin'.
I sit here in a daze.

The flight attendant hands me
Meanest thing that's knowed to man;
A plastic wrapped up snack tray.
It's tougher 'n any can.

That lunch it kind of strikes me
As a irony of life,
'Cause in this flyin' culvert
I don't dare pull a knife.

I've sprained my right front finger
An' now I've broke a tooth
I'm tryin' to reason with it
With words that's some uncouth.

So next I tries my boot heel
I wish I 'as wearin' spurs.
I'd stick this plastic chuck box
Like a blanket full of burrs.

That bit of food just lays there
Safe as gold in old Fort Knox.
Dares me t' try and get it
From that cellophane strong box.

Its saw-toothed knife is packed inside.
Plumb handy, you'll agree.
This plastic slickered little flirt
Just winks and smiles with glee.

But sittin' in the next seat
Is this little tiny kid.
He takes my plate and pats my hand.
One twist, it's all undid.

And while I eats them goodies
I ponders some on life.
I know just what the problem is.
I should 'a' brought my wife.

'Cause, see, she's like that little kid.
It kind of hurts my pride.
These modern day conveniences,
Ain't got them mystified.

But me, I'm plumb shore hog-tied
By this modern day repast.
My wife, she says I'm learnin',
But I ain't learnin' fast.

February

In February,
Tracks in snow
Tell searching eyes
Where wild things go.

The February
Ax blade rings.
Its gray steel tongue
A wood song sings.

In February,
Ice plumes rise
From heated roof
To glacial skies.

The February
Rancher goes
With muffled throat
And frosted nose.

In February,
Frozen words
Hang, chilled in air,
Like crystal birds.

Great Spirit

Almighty Father, hear my prayer.
Each range I cross, I know you're there.
Please watch each switchbacked trail I ride,
And through life's trials, be my guide.

Oh, God, who rules the earth and sky
And numbers bluebirds passing by,
Please help me hunt in every man,
The goodness put there by your hand.

Lord, make me gentle with the old
And when choice comes to good or gold,
Please give me wisdom, then, to seek
What's right before I act or speak.

Great Spirit, as you once were named,
Who ruled before this land was tamed,
When I must cross that Last Divide
Please grant me, Lord, a horse to ride.

You know I'll do just what I'm told,
But I'm not long on streets of gold
And harps, for me, can't match the song
Of nightguards as they ride along.

So when you're makin' up a crew,
To move celestrial longhorns through
The heavens' rangelands up on high,
To that great railhead in the sky.

I'd rather pack my ol' war bag
An' be there, even riding drag,
Than makin' music on a lyre
Or be in some angelic choir.

Amen

Firegod

I have seen him in the rising
Of a far off building storm.
I have heard him in the rumblings
As the thunderheads took form.

I have felt him in the white heat
of a lightning-tortured dawn.
I have smelt his sulf'rous seethings
As the firestorm was spawned.

I have tasted him in ashes
When his maelstromic feast
Left whole forests like the boneyard
of some all-devouring beast.

I still feel him out there circling
Like a wolf that casts about.
For the firegod plays no favorites
As he dogs the trail of drought.

Wolfy Park

The headlines blare the message.
They're searchin' for a park
Where they can introduce the wolf,
A sort of Lobo's Ark.

They're lookin' strong at Yellowstone,
Its swelled up bison herds,
And elk in untold thousands.
The plan's too dumb for words.

See, wolves once stalked the Roche Jaune
But they were plumb distinct.
They cain't just be *re*-introduced
That breed's been long extinct.

There's ranches all around the park
Where men is raisin' beef.
And cow herds meant to feed the world
Is sure to come to grief.

The elk *could* use some cullin',
The buffalo a lot.
Good sense, you say, might raise its head?
Outside the park they're shot?

Well, I've got this suggestion
For Wolfy Habitat.
Let's put them wolves in Central Park
An' see how they like that.

Just think of all them muggers
The whole darn bunch is culls.
Ain't near as fast as runnin' elk
N'r tough as bison bulls.

And benefits to joggers?
They'd plumb improve the breed.
Their wind'd be some better
An' they'd darn sure build their speed.

Them druggies with their needles
Don't know *that* kind of "speed".
They'd be a steady food supply
Help Wolfy Park succeed.

And, maybe, Mayor Dinkins
Could wear his hard hat down
To survey all them wolf kills
In the nation's biggest town.

He'd prob'ly ask for federal aid
To bail 'em out again.
They'd likely ask him for some proof
That wolves is eatin' men.

He'd find plumb quick that wolf lovers
Ain't like them bureaufats.
They've got to see the teeth marks
Or they'll blame it on the rats.

Them wolves'd prosper purty quick
And lose endangered status.
And all them Friends of Animals
Would shore be plumb mad at us.

'Cause, while the wolf's endangered
Their "SAVE THE WOLF" brings cash.
But with them wolves a cullin' man
There'd sure 'nough be a clash.

The wolf is bound to cross the line
Just like in Yellowstone
And if police can't shoot 'em
They'll leave a trail of bone

That even city folks could find
And prob'ly even foller.
'Til purty quick them talk show hosts
Would put up quite a holler.

They'd have them wolves up on the stage
To howl about their rights.
Ol' Oprah'd wring her hands in shame.
Geraldo'd stage some fights.

And Donahue he'd race around
To get the people's views,
And tell how wolves had lost their land
And how they'd been abused.

Rush Limbaugh'd start to giggle
'Bout New Yorkers bein' food.
He'd chuckle out some comments
That some folks'd say was crude.

So put them wolves back in New York
In Boston and L. A.
The District of Columbia
And Frisco by the Bay.

Them places all got lots of parks.
And wolves once lived there, too.
Just think of all the food they'll find
And who'll be eatin' who.

This poem is dedicated to Gary Burnham,
who first suggested the idea.

About the Author

Photo/G.Jill Evans

Mike Logan's poetry is a celebration of the way of life on the ranches of Montana. It was fifteen years of photographing the sometimes gentle, sometimes brutal, always beautiful rhythms of ranch life that led him to begin trying to capture its natural meter and rhyme in words as well as on film.

Logan's poems, though written for fun, are painstakingly crafted. Along the trail they have gained him international recognition as a poet and reciter.

Logan has been a host and featured poet at the Cowboy Poetry Gathering in Elko, Nevada. He has recited his poetry all over the western United States and Canada. Appearing frequently on U.S. and Canadian television, Logan was a featured poet on the 1991 CBS John Denver Christmas Special, "*Montana Christmas Skies.*"

Author and photographer of three books of photography and verse and two books and tapes of cowboy poetry, Mike Logan still views his poetry as just for fun.